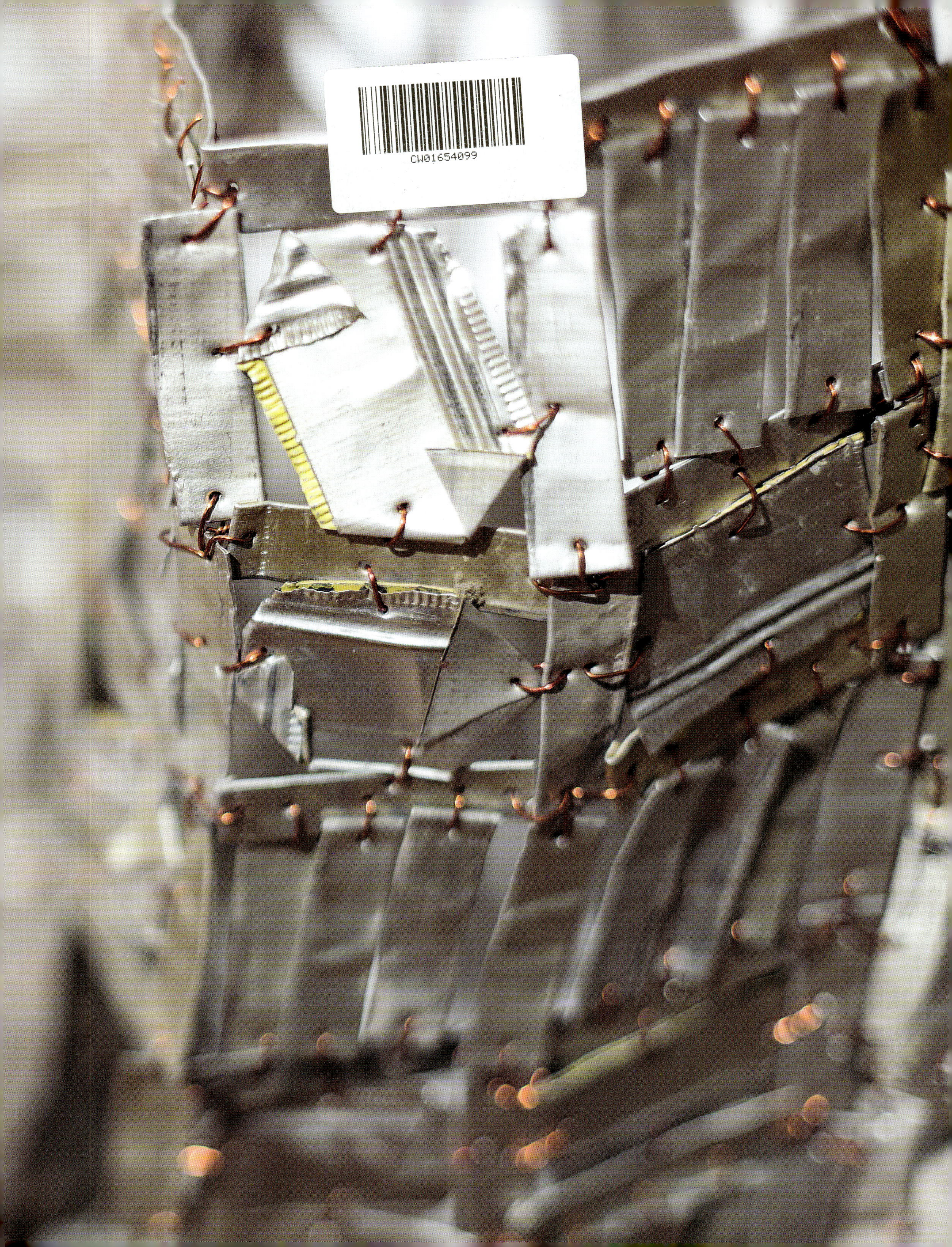

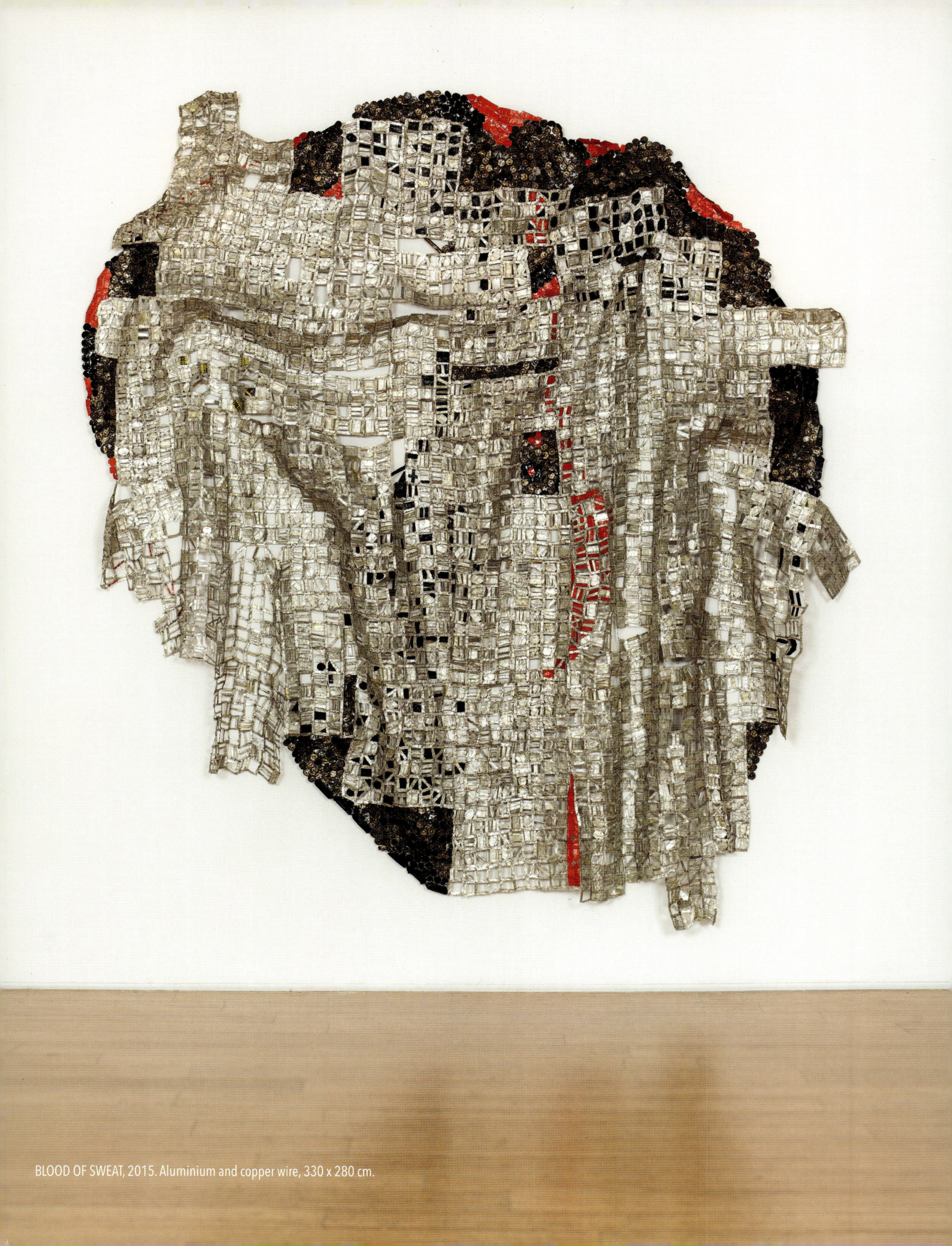

BLOOD OF SWEAT, 2015. Aluminium and copper wire, 330 x 280 cm.

The Nomadic Aesthetic

'I believe that an artwork is something that the viewer, too, should play some positive role in shaping.' – El Anatsui

Opening the sealed wooden crate containing a new 'aluminium bottle-top' work by El Anatsui, evokes a very particular thrill of pleasure. There's a quiver of anticipation: speculations about the form, composition and size of the unknown piece as it gradually emerges. Having now experienced that frisson of expectation so many times, I realise that each and every time, I've been amazed by what materialises. This palpable excitement is shared by everyone helping to lift the carefully folded inner kernel from the crate. There's always surprise, too, at the unexpected lightness of the tightly wrapped package, glittering through its protective shroud like some precious pharaonic gift. First, we unfold it fully, like a large sheet: exposing metal 'fabric' on plastic covering on the gallery's wooden floor. There follows a moment of mutual silence, which no one dares break, as we all stand back to take stock. Unmoving, as though surfacing from sleep, the artwork drinks in the light, passively reflecting back at us our fragmented jumble of first impressions. Even if El Anatsui himself isn't there, at the time, I sense his keen presence. Suddenly, the spell breaks, and we walk around animatedly, surveying it, turning it this way and that, acquainting ourselves with its different aspects until the time comes to fold it back again, wrapped in the darkness of its chest. Then, the instant it disappears from sight, the startled mind plays tricks with the memory, imagining not how it *looked* but how it might *appear* when hung.

Over thirteen years have passed since I first experienced that rush of amazement on opening a crate, from Nigeria, containing the first two metal 'cloths' ever made. We'd shown El Anatsui's work since I first encountered it in the early '90s. In those days, he'd been working primarily in wood with his characteristic *modus operandi* of tearing through tropical hardwoods with a chainsaw, scorching the results and further accentuating the scored wooden surfaces with bright daubs of colour. I thought it powerful, beautiful work, and the gallery exhibited him frequently. I remember, in early 2002, planning with him another show[1] of his latest wall-mounted wood reliefs. Over the phone, almost as an afterthought, he said he wanted to include a couple of works in a 'new metal medium'. He suggested that we could hang them from the ceiling, running down through the centre of the gallery. I needed more details, and since we'd previously mounted one of El's larger installations, comprising hundreds of rusted cassava graters, on the Champs Elysées,[2] I asked if the new works were similar to that. 'Oh No!' came back the laconic reply, 'These are completely different!'

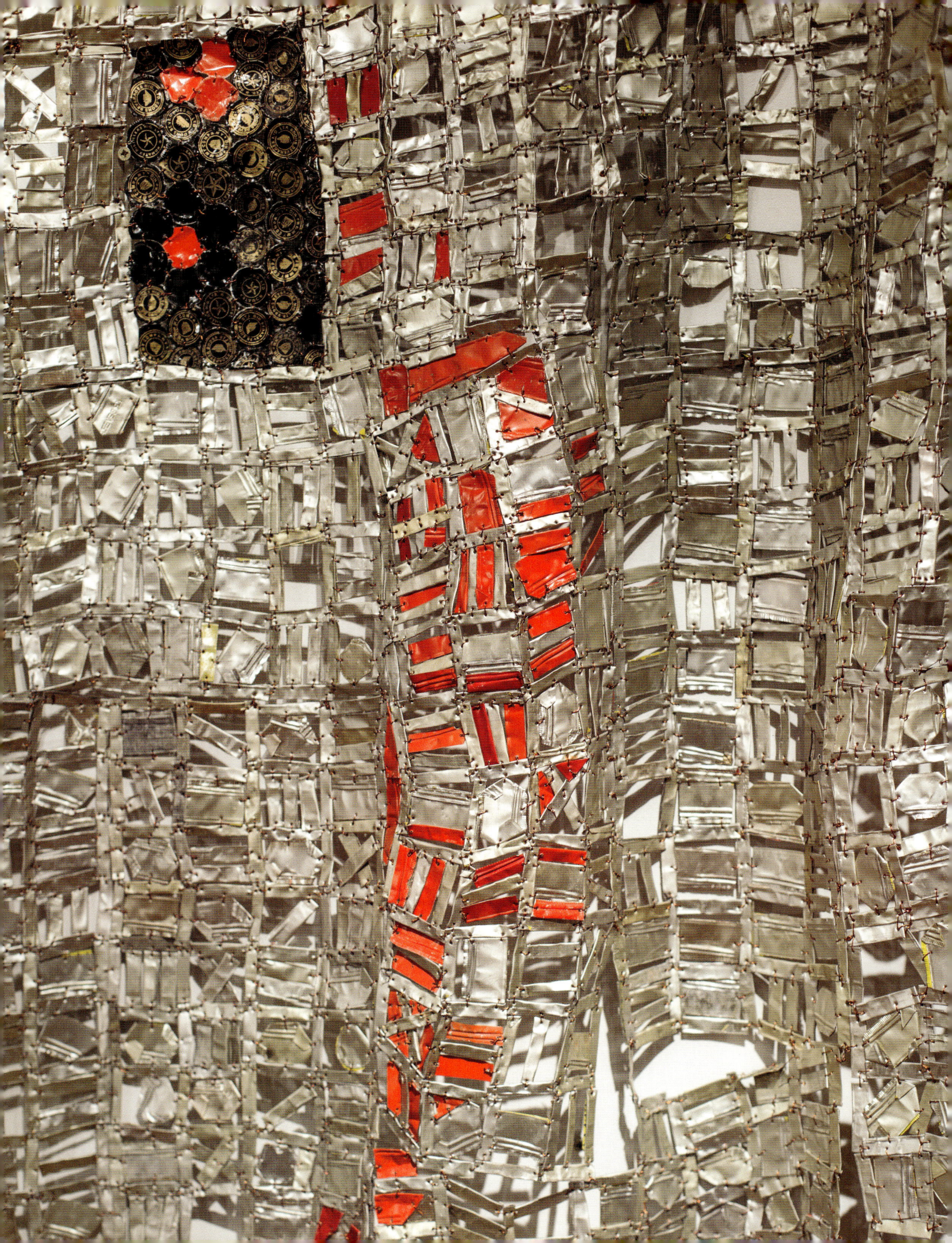

El Anatsui was present for that first unveiling of the 'new metal' pieces in October of 2002. All hands were on deck to unload the unfamiliar cargo. We quickly unwrapped the twin packages within to reveal something that I was delighted to discover was, indeed, completely different from anything I'd ever seen before. I could see how excited El was to be reunited with his 'cloths', and how familiar he was handling the mysterious material. He demonstrated its tensile strength by standing on one corner and tugging, with unrestrained enthusiasm, at the rest. He now wanted the works to hang on the wall, with the smaller, *Woman's Cloth* (2001), more crumpled up and *Man's Cloth* (2001), the larger, given a more evenly distributed fall. Having communicated those few, simple details, El left to go for a walk. I began, with Aliya, my assistant, to learn the secrets of these new materials, trying to give tangible shape to El's ideas. As an artist, I felt an instant affinity for this new form of creation. One quickly becomes intimately acquainted with each cloth, distinguishing the textural differences between them, and such proximity allows those hanging, even for the briefest of times, to make the work their own. After some hours, El returned, made some small adjustments to one piece and pronounced himself satisfied.

When first hung side by side, occupying an entire wall of the gallery, the effect of *Woman's Cloth* and *Man's Cloth* was immediate and unmistakable. More than causing just a stir of interest, they fascinated the public, and collectors soon arrived to view them. The British Museum, not immediately associated with significant acquisitions of contemporary art, were the first in line of several major museums and, having initially placed a reserve on the smaller piece, decided to purchase the historic pair. The significance of El Anatsui's innovative material breakthrough could not have been more cogently confirmed. El later told me that it had taken quite some time, from completing the two original works, for him to decide to exhibit them at all. Whilst investigating how best to display the expansive metal sheets, they'd been hung from the ceiling down the centre of his studio in Nsukka. 'I thought of them as "sculptures" and so my original thinking came from that old-fashioned idea that sculpture was something you had to be able to walk around, not something – like a painting – that you would look at on a wall. Seeing them there in London, I suddenly thought, maybe we should try to hang them on the wall, like the wood wall reliefs. I thought let's just see what happens.'[3] El is never afraid of asking 'what if' questions and taking risks, and he talks about 'letting himself be surprised by possibilities as they unfold'. That impulse to explore, to push beyond material limits and conventional categories, makes him so much the more exciting to work with.

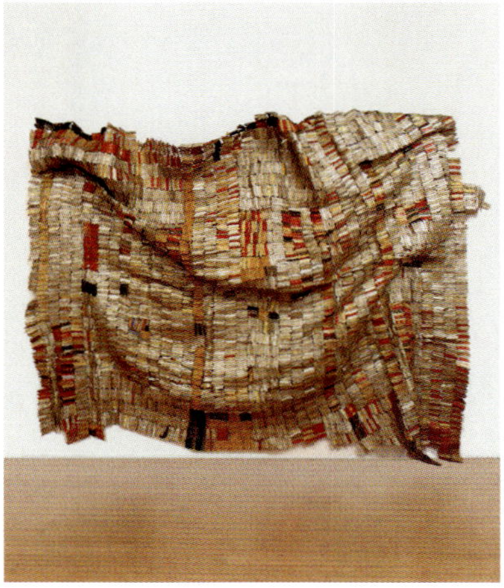

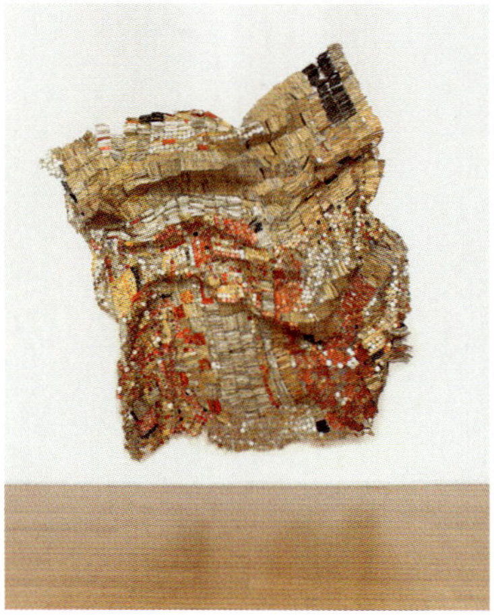

Left: MAN'S CLOTH, 2001.
Aluminium and copper wire, 297 x 374 cm.
Right: WOMAN'S CLOTH, 2001.
Aluminium and copper wire, 287 x 292 cm.
Collection of the British Museum

BLOOD OF SWEAT (detail), 2015. Aluminium and copper wire, 330 x 280 cm.

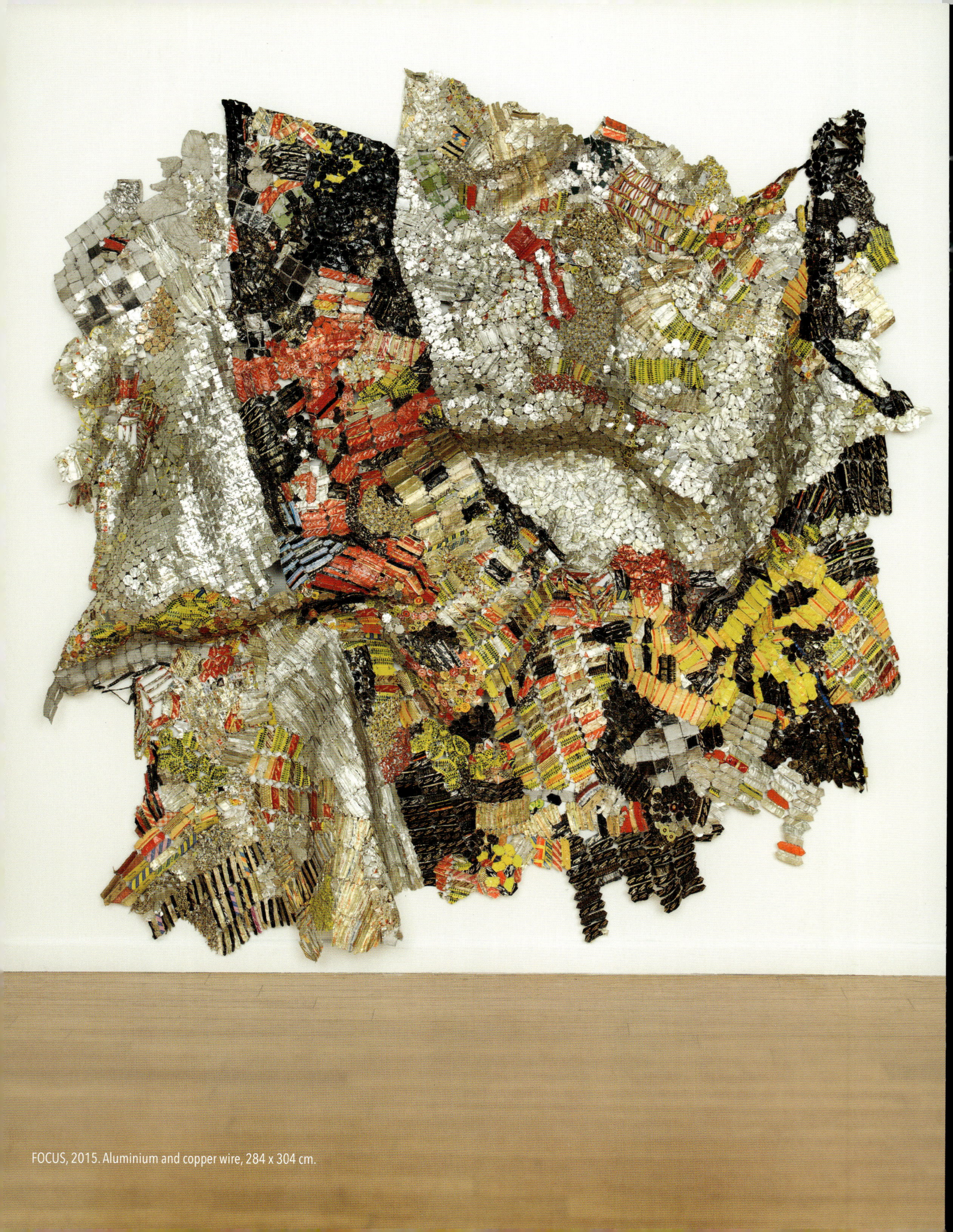

FOCUS, 2015. Aluminium and copper wire, 284 x 304 cm.

Since that first experience of shaping the unknown to give form to an indefinable feeling, I've come to enjoy more and more the bodily experience of the hanging process itself. The tactile connection between the sharp-edged bottle tops linked by twisted copper wires with the hands and arms that shape them is both invigorating and addictive. I'm always conscious of the many individual hands that worked for long hours to 'sew' these metal 'quilts' together, and of the sophisticated consciousness required to organise, control and perfect the entire process before the finished work ever reaches my own hands. My main focus is how to reactivate all that energy and render it visible for others. As I work, I'm searching for a way to bring to life the potential energy of all those individual efforts so that it manifests, dramatically, in movement. Frequently, just as one glimpses a solution as to how a fold might move, the shape slips away and the silhouette vanishes, and no amount of coaxing will ever bring them back. Grappling to impart particular contours to these shifting fabrics reminds me of Eliot's description of wrist-wrestling with words, that:

… sometimes break, under the burden,
Under the tension, slip, slide, perish,
Decay with imprecision, will not stay in place,
Will not stay still.[4]

The definitive 'hang' that is eventually exhibited, results, therefore, from a combination of a steep learning curve pursued down blind alleys, a refusal ever to accept less than one imagines possible and, sometimes, an accidental splash of good fortune. But, for me, that final outcome must bear witness to the drama of the physical engagement itself. I know that my unsung quest mirrors the endless pursuit of the alchemist's dream. However, since the artist has already achieved the impossible task of transforming base metals into luminous sheets of gold, the curator can only dream of displaying those magical transformations boldly, for all to see. If artistically hung and appropriately lit, the amazed spectator might sense the emergent movement in the detailed pattern that captures the illusion of life itself.

In the years following those original cloths, we continued, at first, to refer to all the 'bottle-top' works we received as 'cloths', in part because of the very textile-like properties of the new metal materials. El's long-standing interest in the importance of woven fabrics in the classical African tradition was recorded in earlier pieces like *Sleeping Cloth* (1993 - p.9), *Remnants of Grandma's Cloth* (1995) *and Kente Rhapsody* (2001) even though those pieces were executed in wood. Yet El's constant search for new display strategies and, increasingly, the possibilities of engaging with the challenges of larger museum spaces and the exterior surfaces of buildings, together produced fresh categories of work with no necessary links to 'cloths' at all. So we began simply to refer to them as metal wall relief sculptures. These range from the apparent representation of drawn elements in *Warrior* (2015 - p.22) and *Strained Roots* (2014 - p.26), where the aluminium lozenges operate as pixels that 'paint' recognisable forms, to abstract evocations such as *Timespace* (2014 - p.11) or *Breaking News* (2015 - p.16) that are more conceptual in style. This range of options offers many novel opportunities for display taking into account each work's colour scheme, texture and other formal properties along with any clues suggested by the artist's choice of title.

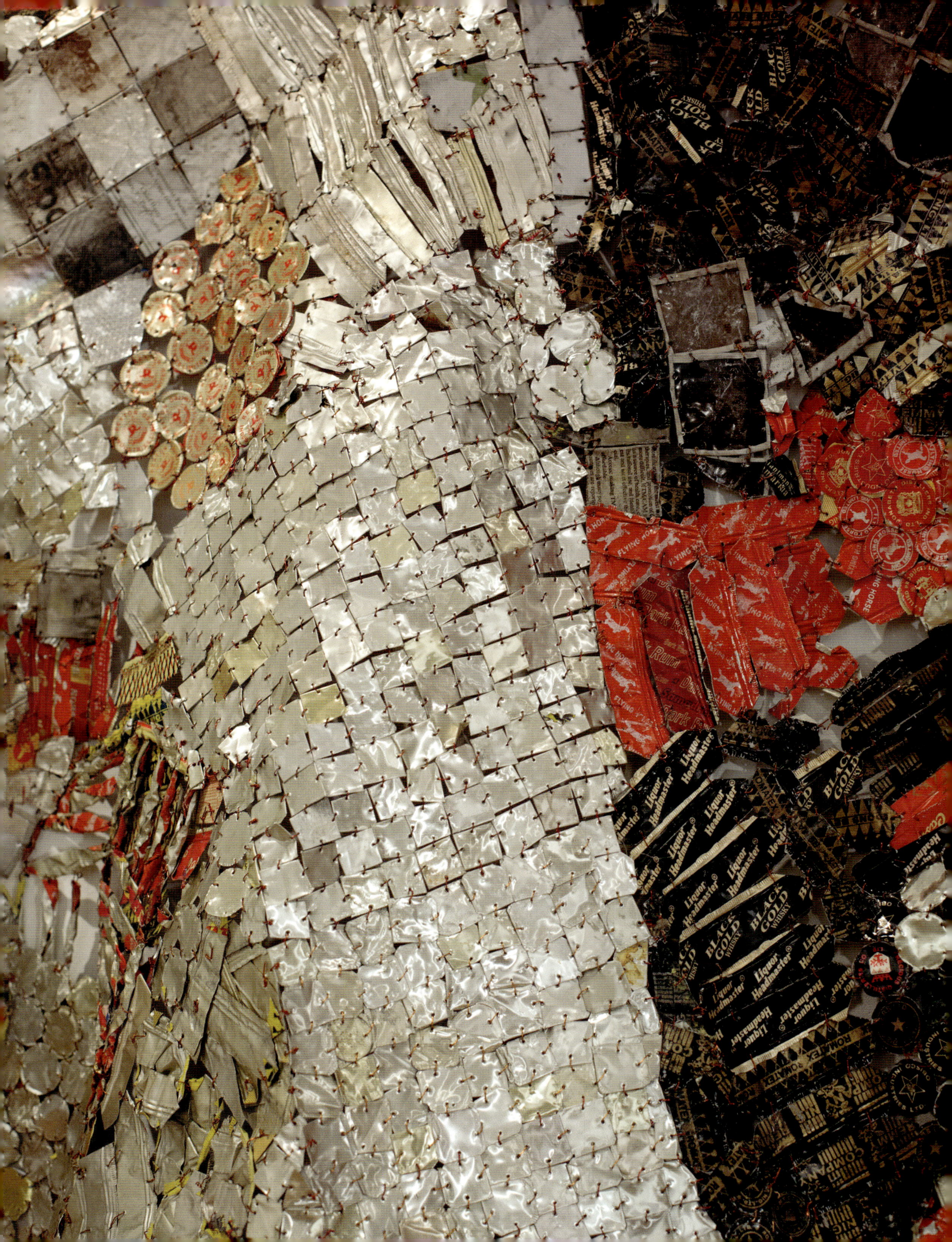
BLACK GOLD
Liquor Headmaster

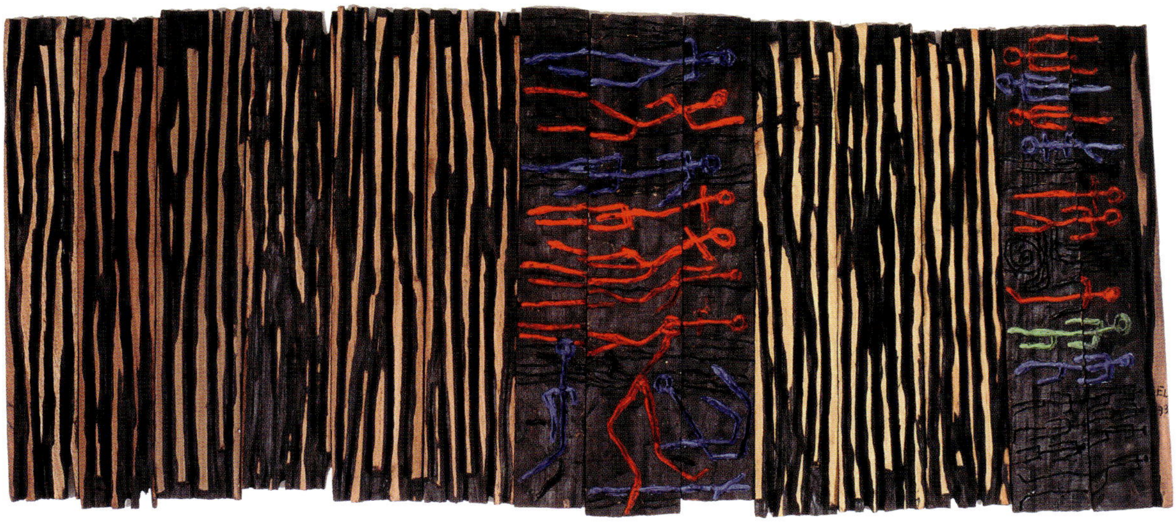

From the curator's perspective, the most liberating aspect of El Anatsui's approach to his work is his daring refusal to prioritise any one interpretation – including that of the artist himself – over any other. Even though he might have encoded a particular message in the work, towards which the title may point, El Anatsui still expects that curators will exercise freedom in hanging the work according to their own vision, and that viewers will still engage with the work from their own point of view. In fact, many of his titles are chosen specifically to open up the possibility of multiple readings, as with, *Dzi I* and *Dzi II* (2015 - p.10 & 20). El Anatsui's native language of Ewe, possesses three tones (high, mid and low) as well as three rising and falling contour tones giving nine possible permutations in total. In common usage, the word dzi has five separate meanings: 'search', 'increase', 'sing', 'give birth' and 'heart', with each one distinguished by a variant in pitch and tone. Since the artist has attached no specific tonal register to either work, all five meanings are possible readings, at one and the same time, for both pieces. Such freedom is a fundamental feature of El Anatsui's way of operating: be it the freedom from prescribed ideas and fixed categories; the freedom to work with whatever the environment throws up; the freedom to explore all the implications of a new medium or the freedom to reconfigure or reinterpret a work completely. It is a rare artist who is sufficiently confident in the power of his creations that he approves of - indeed expects - a diversity of strategies for visual display as well as a plurality of possible readings.

In part this aspect of his practice grows out of El Anatsui's own experience of having to exhibit ever more frequently overseas. Following the 44th Venice Biennale in 1990, he found himself, within a brief five-year period, exhibiting in: Germany, the U.K., the U.S.A., Italy, Cuba, Brazil, South Africa, Sweden and Switzerland, and at multiple venues in each country. Comparing his experience to those nomadic peoples, who move around from place to place, constantly interacting with different cultural groups and always dependent upon their ability to pack up quickly and move on, he began to think loosely about 'the aesthetic of the nomad' as a way of describing his constant necessity of shipping crates of artworks around the world, sometimes to locations where he was unable to mount the work in person. In such situations he was sometimes dependent on unknown curators to place his work, others to interpret it and ultimately, to those viewers in far-off places to derive whatever 'messages' they could. Problems that might have troubled many, however, played to his strengths. He understood that an obvious reference to an African observer might mean little at all, or

Left: FOCUS (detail), 2015. Aluminium and copper wire, 284 x 304 cm.
Above: SLEEPING CLOTH,1993. Tropical hardwoods and tempera, 61 x 145 cm.

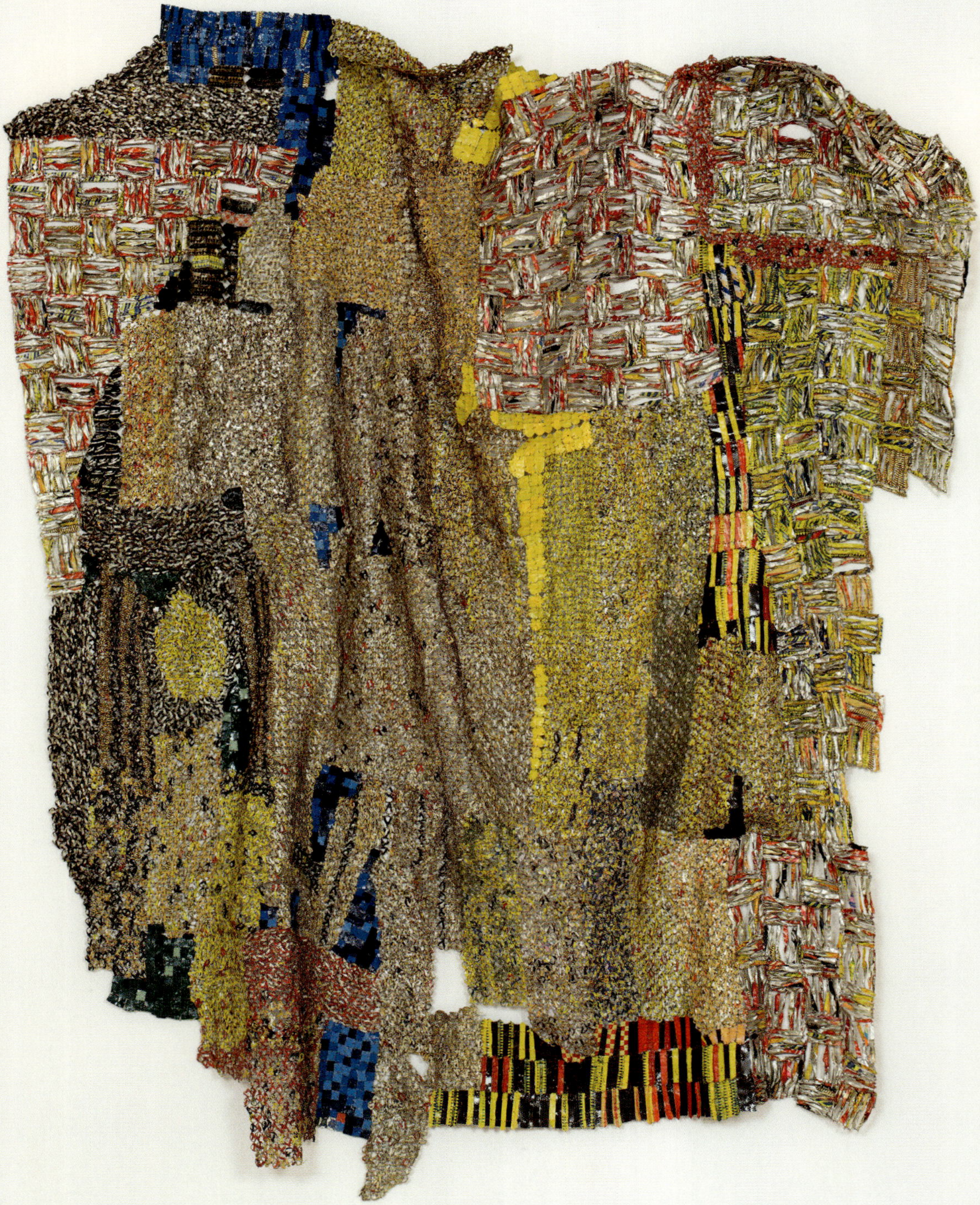

DZI I, 2015. Aluminium and copper wire, 288 x 258 cm.

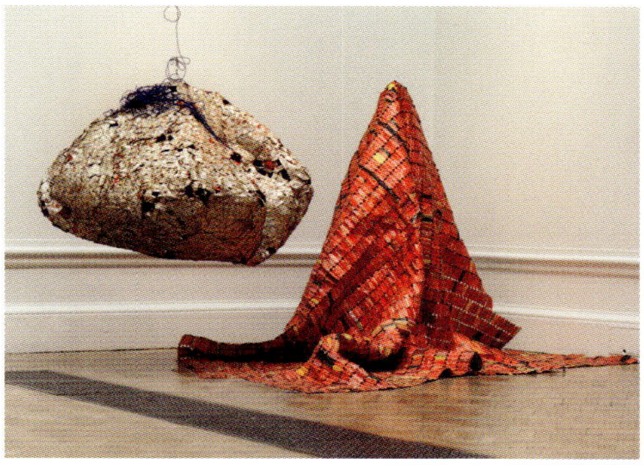 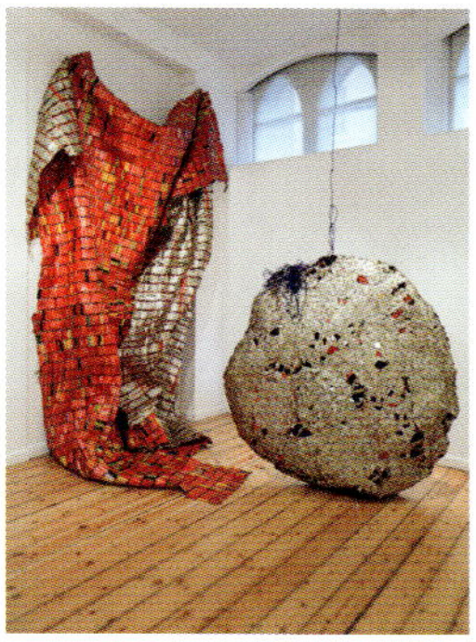 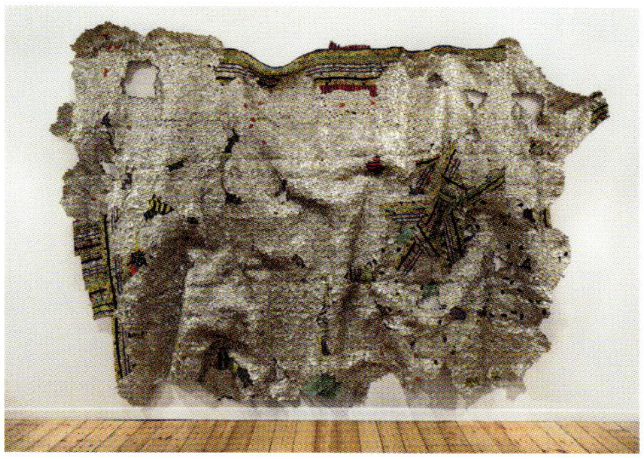

have different associations again in Japan. 'You don't give cut-and-dried statements to others; and you can't assume that people don't have the ability to derive their own statements from the artwork. In other words, I want people to play around and derive their own meanings.'[5] The wood wall reliefs already contained, in embryonic form, a shape-shifting facility allowing for different modes of display. Curators were encouraged to change the relative positions of the individual panels of wood, which were free to move, and develop new configurations, alternative arrangements that might be hung at variable heights or spaced differently apart. Consequent upon the possibility of physical re-arrangement comes the notion that any 'meaning' integral to the work is a similarly plastic concept, open to variation. These radical ideas are, perhaps, best left to the artist himself to describe:

> 'The idea of the nomadic aesthetic has something to do with the kind of media that I was using, which were light and easy to move about. This means my thinking remains fluid. Conceptually, this kind of aesthetic means, that you have the freedom to do anything you want with the work. You can change it about, you can bundle it up, or fold it down, and the fact that you can do all these things also affects the aesthetics of the works themselves. You can change the pieces around and you can go to new locations with them. Even though the materials themselves don't change, you can create something new each time you hang them.'[6]

Though a feature seldom explored by curators of the earlier wood wall reliefs, this potential for variation became an intrinsic property of all the works produced using the mutable fabrics of the new metal medium. Here, the nature of the material determines that the curator must become an interpreter in hanging or otherwise installing the work. Each installation of any single work is a one-off event: every re-installation will be different again, and, hence, similarly unique. A work like *AG+BA* (2014 - above), first exhibited at the Royal Academy of Arts Summer Exhibition, which plays with relationships between a simple 'sheet' of material and a more sculpturally determined 'object', provides a good example. Each view, any perspective and every image of the work, in its several manifestations to date, presents entirely different aspects of the interaction between the two discrete parts. The same is likewise true of all other 'bottle-top' works now being transported from one exhibition to another around the globe. This Heraclitan paradox, of being unable to step into the same river twice, became apparent from the outset. *Man's Cloth* was re-hung for the very first time, in March, 2003, for an opening designed to display the recent acquisition, in the African Galleries of the British Museum. All attempts to recreate the impressive folds and dramatic sweep of the original 'hang' proved impossible to achieve without the construction of a purpose-built frame to fix the quicksilver material in place. Yet, even then, the location, the setting and the critical elements of

Above left & centre: AG+BA, 2014. Royal Academy of Art, London (2014), October Gallery, London (2015).
Aluminium, copper wire and nylon string, size variable.
Above right: TIMESPACE, 2014. Aluminium and copper wire, 325 x 495 cm.

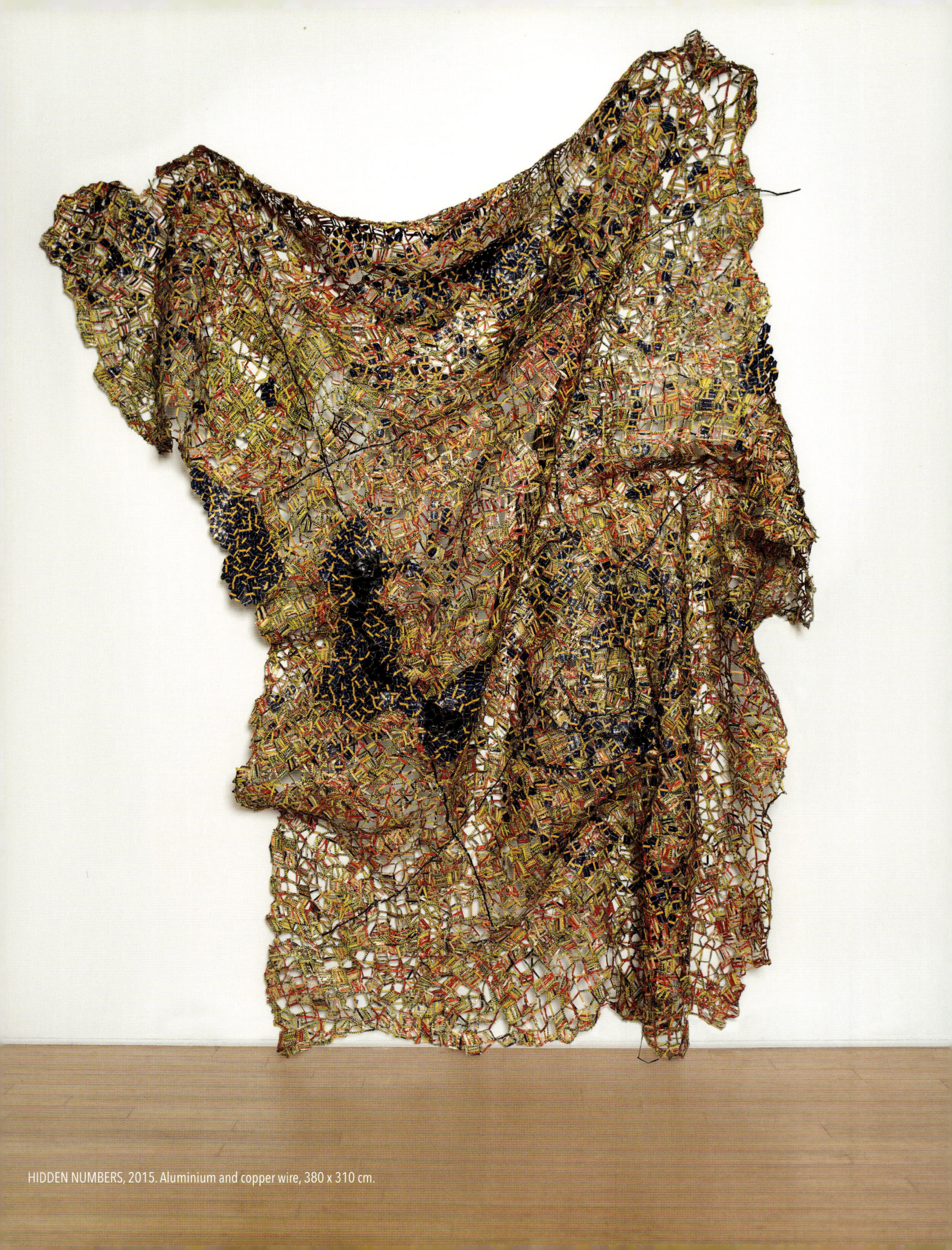

HIDDEN NUMBERS, 2015. Aluminium and copper wire, 380 x 310 cm.

lighting and shade – all prime essentials on which the work thrives – were different, as – inevitably – was the overall effect. Today, this proud, shimmering masterpiece remains on permanent display, and is the vital first thing that greets every visitor who enters the African Galleries.

Around 2007, as technical improvements in new ways of folding and linking the bottle tops developed, the materials became capable of bearing even greater weights at larger scales, and the display horizons began to expand exponentially. As ever-larger works were created they began to migrate from the interior walls of galleries and museums to exterior locations. In that year, whilst a pair of immense works hung inside the Arsenale at the Venice Biennale, another large-scale work was draped over the front elevation of the Palazzo Fortuny. Successively larger installations have continued to be produced in recent years, of which the largest 'bottle-top' piece, to date, is *Tsiatsia - searching for connection* (2013 - p.14). This monumental work, measuring over 4,000 square feet in total, bedecked the facade of the Royal Academy of Arts, in London, in the Summer of 2013. Designed to fit precisely within the central area above the portico of Burlington House, and to be framed architecturally by the two adjoining wings, the work was admired by many thousands of visitors.

But this magnificent piece was also designed in accordance with the principles of the nomadic aesthetic. Having taken over a year to create, it folds down and packs away into four medium-sized crates within a matter of hours. These crates unpack to give eight individual 'panels' that, when hung, can then be connected in *situ* to re-create the complete work. Together with the material's inherent ability to transform, both in size and shape, when eventually transported to another venue its chameleon-like properties ensure that it will appear as a completely new work, adapting itself to its new environment as though designed for nothing else. Those eight panels can be reconfigured: hung in an altered sequence, sideways, reversed or intertwined according to the demands of the site and the open-ended vision of the artist, or his delegated curator, *sur place*. In accordance with that freedom proper to the nomadic aesthetic, deeply inscribed in the cellular structures of the work, that yet-to-be realised installation of the future will be susceptible to as many alternative interpretations as there are spectators who will be amazed by what materialises.

Elisabeth Lalouschek, Artistic Director, October Gallery, 2016.

1 El Anatsui: *Recent Works*, 2002, October Gallery, London.
2 El Anatsui, *Ancient Wall*, 1999, Paris, 'Les Champs de la Sculpture.'
3 El Anatsui, in personal communication to author in an interview conducted in 2014.
4 T. S. Eliot. *Four Quartets: Burnt Norton, V*, 1941
5 El Anatsui, in personal communication, in an interview at October Gallery, in 2005.
6 El Anatsui, in personal communication to author in an interview conducted in 2014.

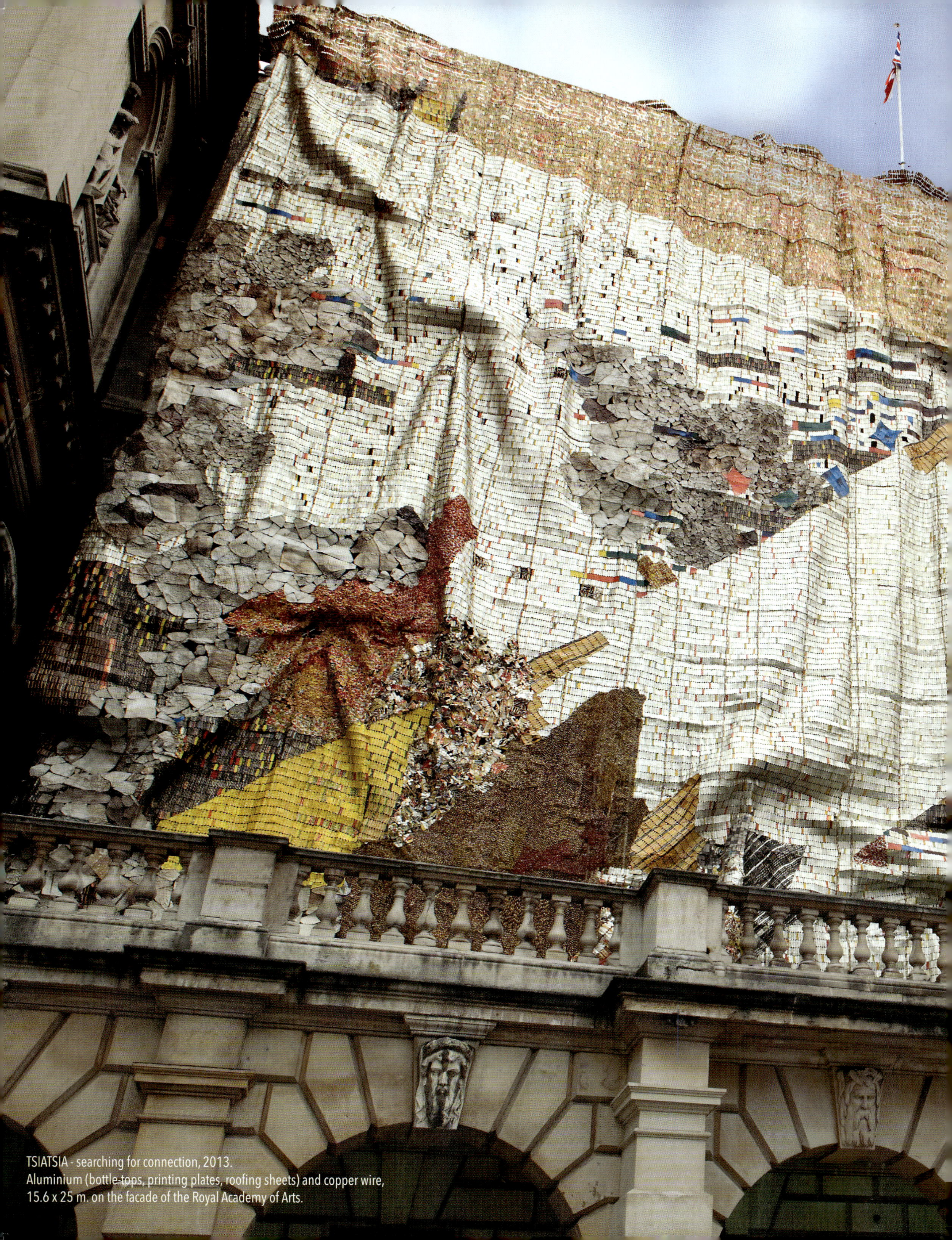

TSIATSIA - searching for connection, 2013.
Aluminium (bottle-tops, printing plates, roofing sheets) and copper wire,
15.6 x 25 m. on the facade of the Royal Academy of Arts.

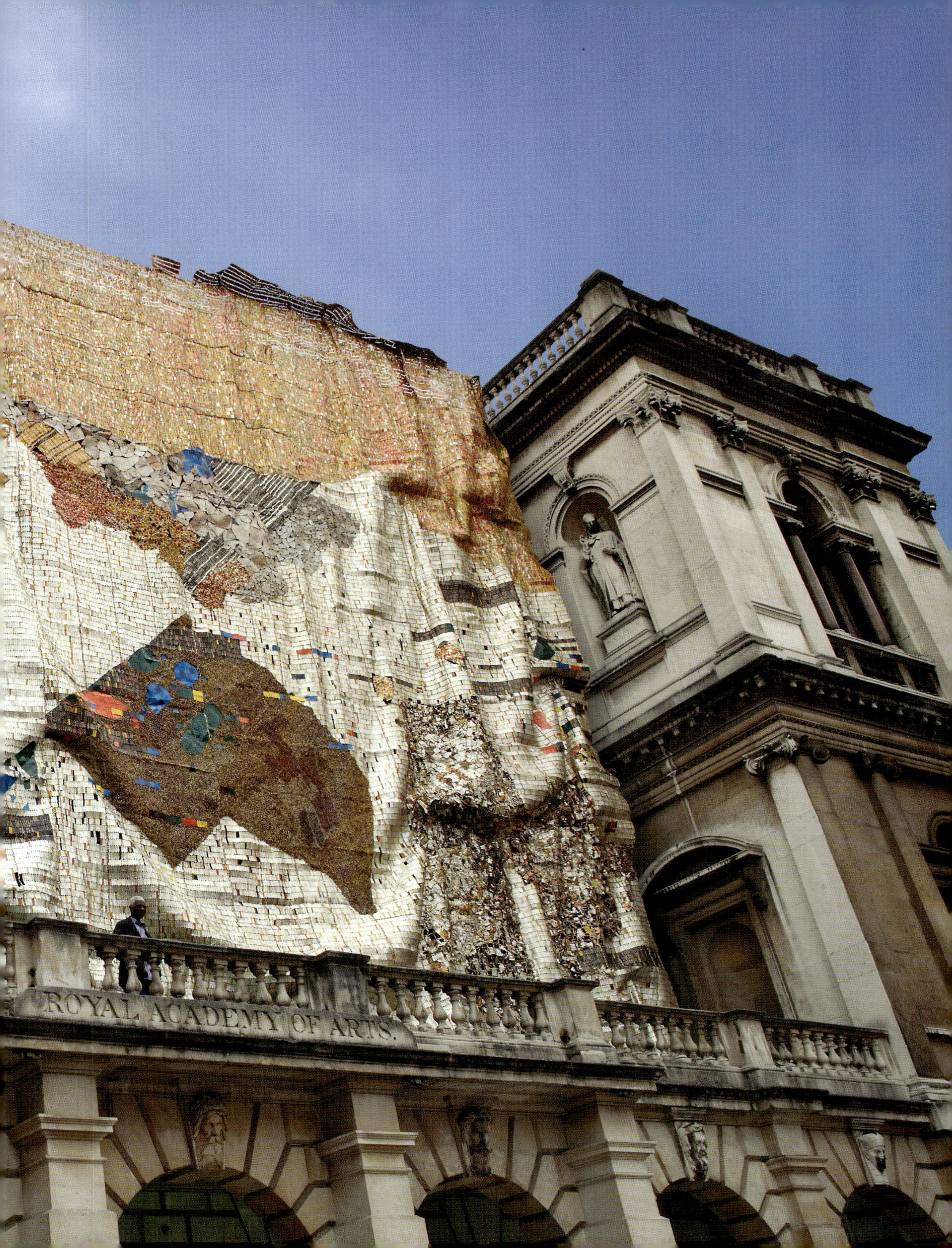
ROYAL ACADEMY OF ARTS

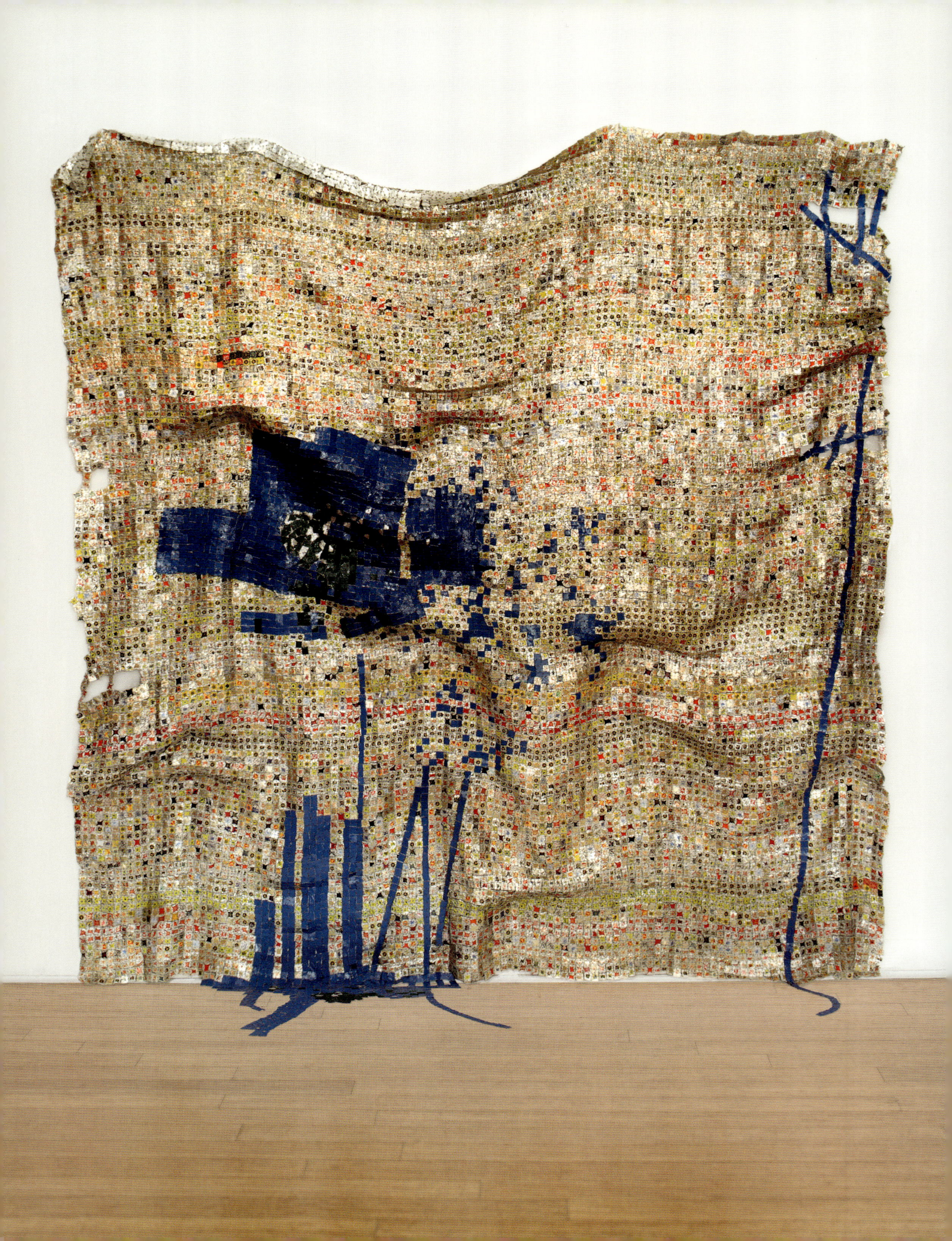

BREAKING NEWS, 2015. Aluminium and copper wire, 326 x 264 cm.

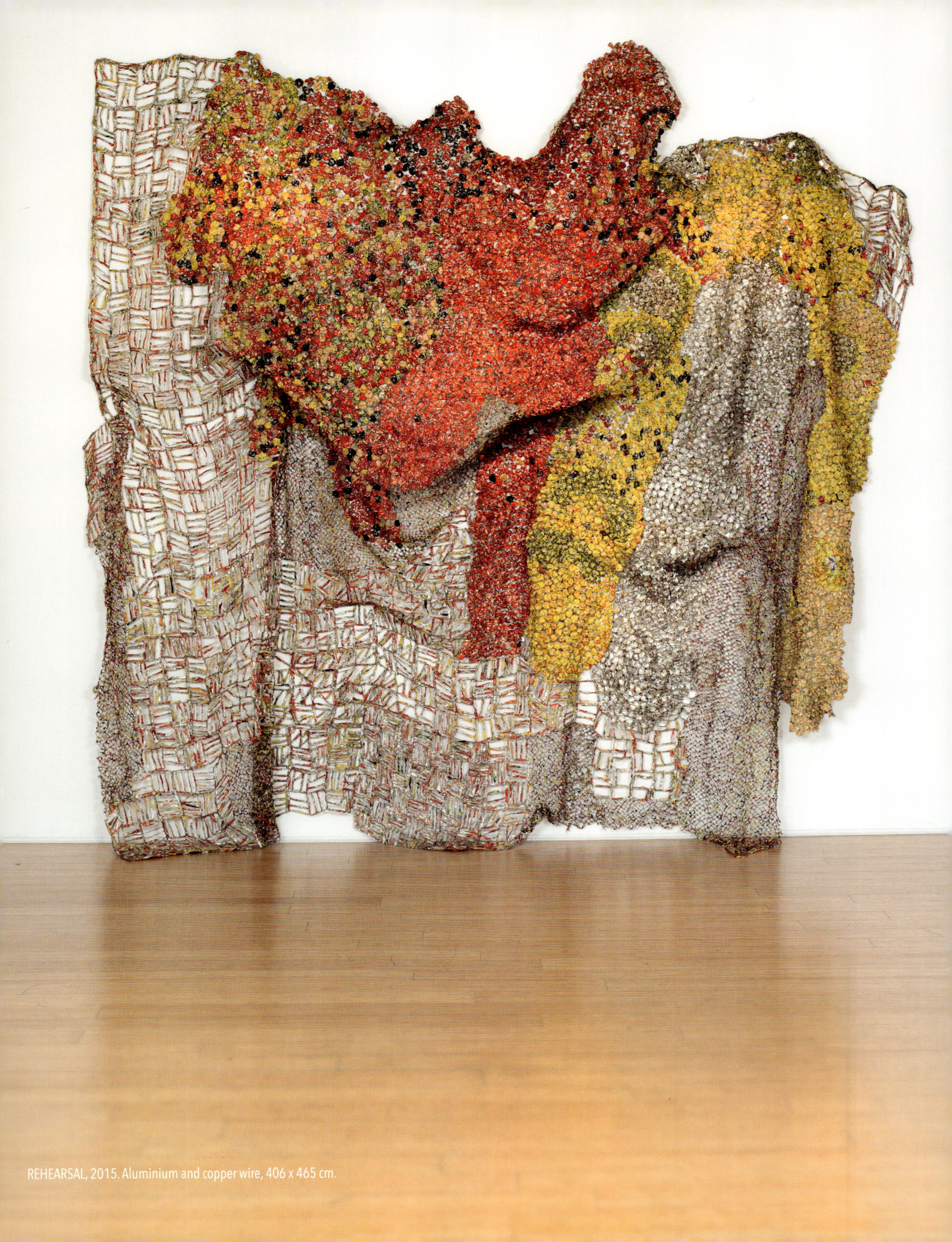

REHEARSAL, 2015. Aluminium and copper wire, 406 x 465 cm.

El Anatsui

Born in 1944, Ghana.
Lives and works between Ghana and Nigeria.
In 2014 he was made an Honorary Royal Academician as well as elected into the American Academy of Arts and Sciences.

Education

1969
Postgraduate Diploma, Art Education, Kwame Nkrumah University of Science and Technology (KNUST), Kumasi, Ghana

1965 - 1969
B.A. College of Art, Kwame Nkrumah University of Science and Technology (KNUST), Kumasi, Ghana

Major Awards

2015
Golden Lion for Lifetime Achievement of the 56th International Art Exhibition of the Biennale di Venezia – *All the World's Futures*, Venice, Italy

2013
Charles Wollastan Award of the Royal Academy of Arts, London, UK

Solo Exhibitions

2016
El Anatsui: New Works, October Gallery, London, UK
El Anatsui: Five Decades, Carriageworks, Sydney Festival 2016, Sydney, Australia

2015
El Anatsui, October Gallery, London, UK
El Anatsui: Five Decades, Jack Shainman Gallery - The School, Kinderhook, New York, USA
El Anatsui of Dzi, Kunstbanken Hedmark Kunstsenter, Hamar, Norway

2014
El Anatsui – Theory of Se, Axel Vervoordt Gallery, Hong Kong
El Anatsui: Playing with Chance, Centre for Contemporary Art, Lagos, Nigeria
El Anatsui: New Worlds, Mount Holyoke College, South Hadley, Massachusetts, USA
El Anatsui: Trains of Thought, Jack Shainman Gallery, New York, USA
El Anatsui, Mnuchin Gallery, New York, USA

2012 - 2015
Gravity and Grace: Monumental Works by El Anatsui, Akron Art Museum, Akron, Ohio; Brooklyn Museum, New York; Des Moines Art Center, Iowa; Bass Museum of Art, Miami, USA; Museum of Contemporary Art San Diego, USA

2012
Pot of Wisdom, Jack Shainman Gallery, New York, USA
Stitch in Time, Axel Vervoordt Gallery, Antwerp, Belgium

2011
El Anatsui, Sterling and Francine Clark Art Institute, Williamstown, Massachusetts, USA

2010 - 2012
El Anatsui: When I Last Wrote To You About Africa, organised by the Museum for African Art, New York, USA; Royal Ontario Museum, Toronto, Canada; Davis Museum, Wellesley College, Wellesley, Massachusetts; Blanton Museum of Art, University of Texas, Austin; North Carolina Museum of Art, Raleigh, North Carolina; Denver Art Museum, Colorado; University of Michigan Museum of Art, Ann Arbor, Michigan, USA

2010 - 2011
A Fateful Journey, National Museum of Ethnology, Osaka; The Museum of Modern Art, Hayama; Tsuruoka Art Forum, Tsuruoka Art, The Museum of Modern Art, Saitama, Japan

2010
Gli, Rice University Art Gallery, Houston, Texas, USA
El Anatsui, Jack Shainman Gallery, New York, USA

2009
El Anatsui, Belger Arts Center, Kansas City, Missouri, USA
Process and Project, BRIC Rotunda Gallery, Brooklyn, New York, USA

2008
Earth Growing Roots, San Diego State University Art Gallery, San Diego, USA
Zebra Crossing, Jack Shainman Gallery, New York, USA

2006
Asi, David Krut Projects, New York, USA, in collaboration with October Gallery, London, UK
Nyekor, Spazio Rossana Orlandi, Milan, Italy, in collaboration with October Gallery, London, UK

2005
Danudo: Recent Sculptures of El Anatsui, Skoto Gallery in collaboration with Contemporary African Art Gallery, New York, USA

2003 - 2008
El Anatsui: Gawu, Oriel Mostyn Gallery, Llandudno, Wales, UK; Model Arts & Niland Gallery, Sligo, Ireland; Gallery Oldham, Oldham; October Gallery, London; Djanogly Art Gallery, University of Nottingham, UK; Samuel P. Harn Museum of Art, Gainesville, Florida; Hood Museum of Art, Dartmouth College, Hanover, New Hampshire; Fowler Museum, University of California, Los Angeles; University of Arizona Museum of Art, Tucson; The National Museum of African Art, Smithsonian Institution, Washington, D.C., USA

2002
New Works, October Gallery, London, UK

1998
A Sculpted History of Africa, October Gallery, London, UK

2012 - 2013
Broken Bridge II, the High Line, New York, USA

1997
Hakpa, French Cultural Centre, Lagos, Nigeria

1995
El Anatsui: Sculptures and Reliefs, October Gallery, London, UK

1991
Old and New: An Exhibition of Sculpture in Assorted Wood, National Museum, Lagos, Nigeria

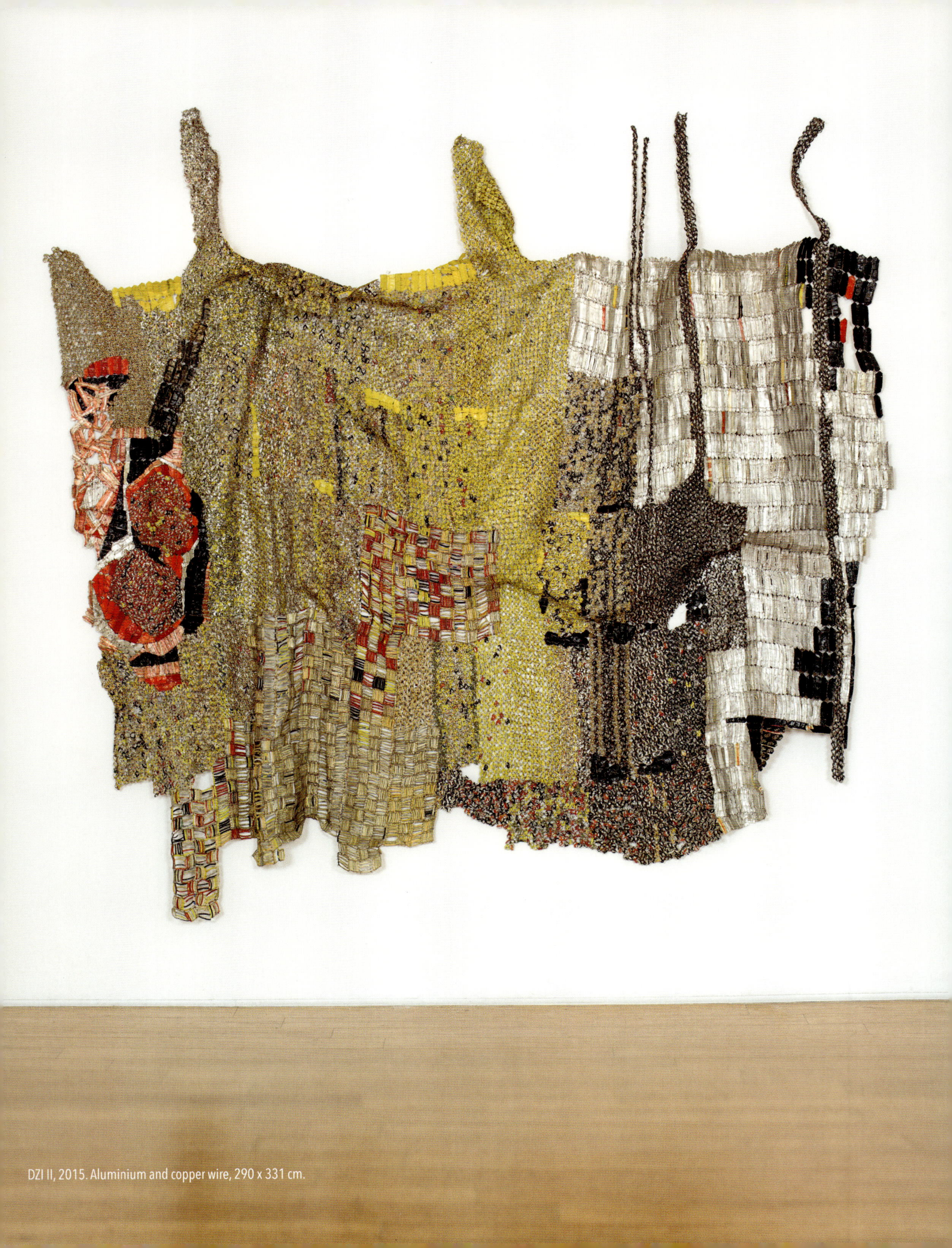

DZI II, 2015. Aluminium and copper wire, 290 x 331 cm.

1987

Pieces of Wood: An Exhibition of Mural Sculpture, The Franco-German Auditorium, Lagos, Nigeria

1982

Sculptures, Photographs, Drawings, Goethe-Institut, Lagos, Nigeria

1980

Wood Carvings, Cummington Community of Arts, Cummington, Massachusetts, USA

1979

Broken Pots: Sculpture by El Anatsui, British Council, Enugu, Nigeria; Institute of African Studies, University of Nigeria, Nsukka, Nigeria

1976

Wooden Wall Plaques, Asele Art Gallery, Nsukka, Nigeria

Group Exhibitions

2016

Marrakech Biennale 6; Not New Now, Marrakech, Morocco

2015

Africa Africans, Museu Afro Brazil, São Paulo, Brazil
Field, Road, Cloud: Art and Africa, Anna K. Meredith Gallery, Des Moines Art Center, Des Moines, Iowa, USA
Embracing Space and Color: Art On & Off the Wall, Vero Beach Museum of Art, USA
Meet Me Halfway: Selections from the Anita Reiner Collection, Cristin Tierney Gallery, Florida, USA
Re:Purposed, The John & Mable Ringling Museum of Art, State Art Museum of Florida, Florida State University, Sarasota, Florida, USA
Piece Work, Yale University School of Art, New Haven, Connecticut, USA
Summer Exhibition 2015, Royal Academy of Arts, London, UK
Atopolis, Wiels in collaboration with Mons 2015, Manège de Sury, Mons, Belgium
PROPORTIO, Palazzo Fortuny, Venice, Italy

2014

Mise En Scène, The School, Kinderhook, NY, USA
The Art of Our Time: Masterpieces from the Guggenheim Collections, Guggenheim Bilbao, Spain

2013

245th Summer Exhibition, installation of sculpture on the facade of the Royal Academy of Arts, London, UK
ArtZuid 2013, Amsterdam, The Netherlands
Masters of the Transvangarde, October Gallery, London, UK
Earth Matters: Land as Material and Metaphor in the Arts of Africa, National Museum of African Art, Smithsonian Institution, Washington, D.C., USA

2012

El Gran Sur, 1st Montevideo Biennial, Montevideo, Uruguay
All Our Relations, 18th Biennale of Sydney, Sydney, Australia
Intense Proximity, Paris Triennial 2012, Palais de Tokyo/ Musée Galliera, Paris, France
African Cosmos: Stellar Art, National Museum of African Art, Smithsonian Institution, Washington, D.C., USA
Dialogues, Setagaya Art Museum, Tokyo, Japan
We Face Forward, Manchester Art Gallery, Manchester, UK
Architectural Environments for Tomorrow: New Spatial Practices in Architecture and Art, Museum of Contemporary Art Tokyo, Tokyo University of the Arts, Tokyo, Japan

2011 - 2012

Environment and Object: Recent African Art, Frances Young Tang Teaching Museum and Art Gallery at Skidmore College, New York; Anderson Gallery, Virginia Commonwealth University, Richmond; Middlebury College Museum of Art, Middlebury, Vermont, USA

2011

The World Belongs to You, Palazzo Grassi, Venice, Italy
ARS 11, Museum of Contemporary Art Kiasma, Helsinki, Finland
Hunters and Gatherers: The Art of Assemblage, Sotheby's, New York, USA
The Splendour of Truth, The Beauty of Charity, The Vatican, Rome, Italy

2010

Who Knows Tomorrow, Alte Nationalgalerie, Berlin, Germany
Human Rites, Bass Museum of Art, Miami Beach, Florida, USA
A Collective Diary, an African Contemporary Journey, Herzilya Museum of Contemporary Art, Herzilya, Israel

2009

Against Exclusion, 3rd Moscow Biennale, Moscow, Russia
Intramoenia Extra Art, Castelli di Puglia, Barletta Castle, Barletta, Ital
Chance Encounters: Seven Contemporary African Artists, Sakshi Gallery, Mumbai, India
Transvangarde: Leading Contemporary Artists, October Gallery, London, UK
Confines Extremos. Confines Urbanos, Institut Valencia D'Art Modern, Valencia, Spain
Off the Grid, Belger Arts Center, Kansas City, Missouri, USA
Homecoming, Artists Alliance Gallery, Accra, Ghana
Promoter-of- Nigerian-Art Series, Goethe Institute, Lagos, Nigeria
Embrace! Denver Art Museum, Colorado, USA

2008

Second Lives: Remixing the Ordinary, Museum for Arts and Design, New York, USA
The Poetics of Cloth: African Textiles, Grey Art Gallery, New York, USA
The Essential Art of African Textiles: Design Without End, The Metropolitan Museum of Art, New York, USA
Second Lives: Remixing the Ordinary, Museum for Arts and Design, New York, USA
World Histories, Des Moines Art Center, Des Moines, Iowa, USA *Angaza Afrika: African Art Now*, October Gallery, London, UK
Recycling: The Whole House, Kunstbanken Hedmark Kunstsenter, Hamar, Norway
Juego Africano de lo Contemporáneo: Pre-figuraciones Postcoloniales, Museo de Arte Contemporáneo Unión Fenosa (MACUF), A Coruña, Spain
Prospect.1 New Orleans, New Orleans, Louisiana, USA
Sonsbeek 2008: Grandeur, Sonsbeek Park, Arnhem, The Netherlands

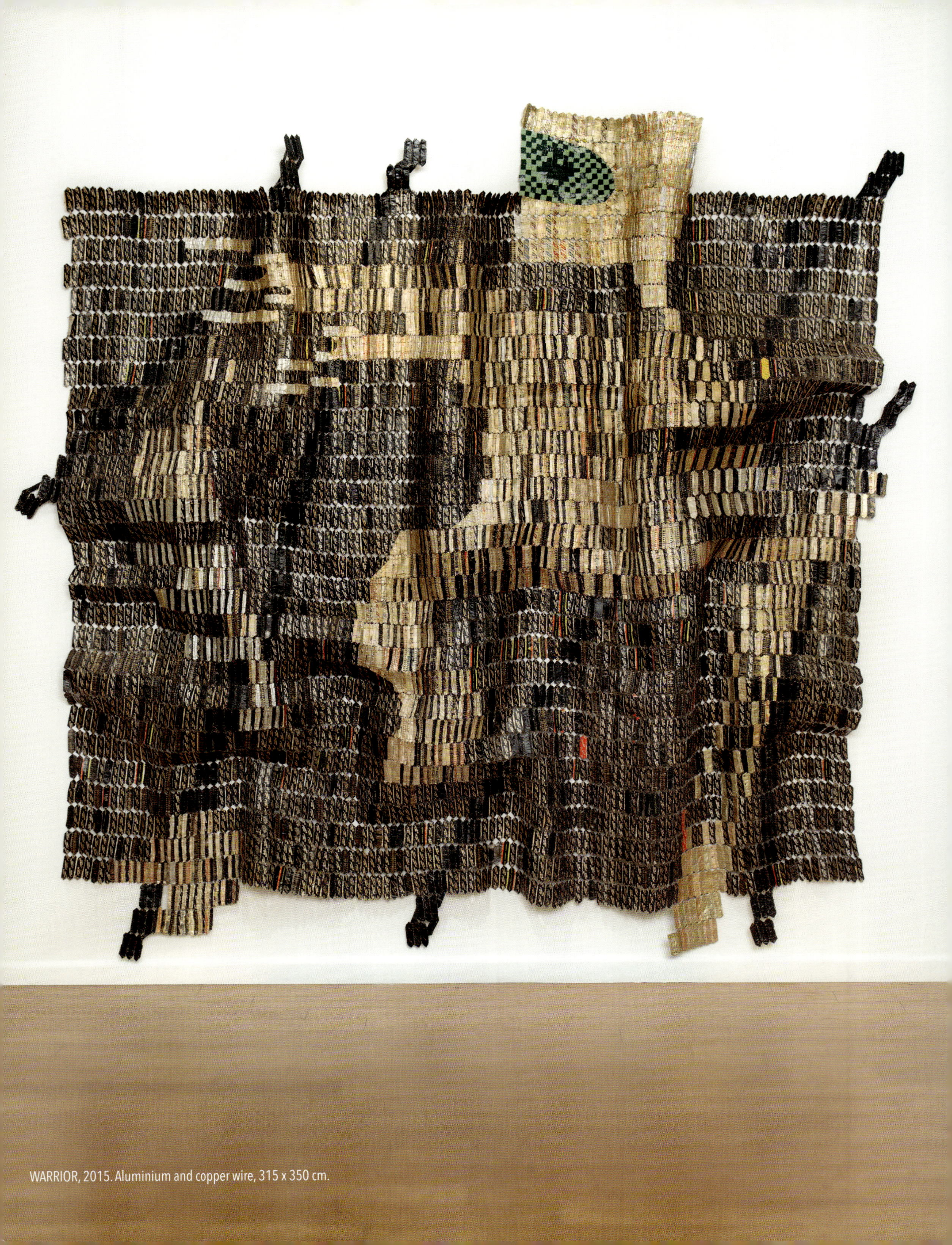

WARRIOR, 2015. Aluminium and copper wire, 315 x 350 cm.

2007

Tapping Currents: Contemporary African Art and the Diaspora, The Nelson-Atkins Museum of Art, Kansas City, Missouri, USA
Un/Fair Trade: The Art of Justice, Neue Galerie, Graz; Landesmuseum Joanneum, Styria, Austria
From Courage to Freedom, October Gallery, London, UK
Living Masters, Terra Culture, Lagos, Nigeria
The Boys Craft, Haifa Museum of Art, Haifa, Israel
Still Life: Art, Ecology, and the Politics of Change, 8th Sharjah Biennial, UAE

2006 - 2011

The Missing Peace: Artists Consider the Dalai Lama, UCLA Fowler Museum of Cultural History, Los Angeles, California; Loyola University Museum of Art, Chicago, Illinois; Rubin Museum of Art, New York; Visual Arts Gallery, Emory University, Atlanta, Georgia; Yerba Buena Center for the Arts, San Francisco, California, USA; Hillside Terrace Galleries, Daikanyama, Tokyo, Japan; Fundación Canal, Madrid, Spain; The Patricia and Phillip Frost Art Museum, Florida International University, Miami, Florida, USA; Brukenthal National Museum, Sibiu, Romania; Nobel Museum, Stockholm, Sweden; San Antonio Museum of Art, Texas, USA

2006

Altered, Stitched and Gathered, MoMA PS1, New York, USA
DAK'ART 2006, 7th Biennale of African Art, Dakar, Senegal
-poiesis, Jack Shainman Gallery, New York, USA
Europe-Afrique: Regards Croisés, Ateliers des Tanneurs, Brussels, Belgium *Black Panther Rank and File*, Yerba Buena Center for the Arts, San Francisco, USA *Primitivsm Revisited: After the End of an Idea*, Sean Kelly Gallery, New York, USA
Expanding Africa: New Art, New Directions, Newark Museum, Newark, New Jersey, USA
Body of Evidence, National Museum of African Art, Smithsonian Institution, Washington, D.C., USA

2005

In the Making: Materials and Process, Michael Stevenson Gallery, Cape Town, South Africa
Out There, Sainsbury Centre for the Visual Arts, Norwich, UK
AKA . . . of Age 2005, Maison de France, Lagos, Nigeria
De Young Museum, San Francisco, USA

2004 - 2007

Afrika Remix, Museum Kunstpalast, Düsseldorf, Germany; Hayward Gallery, London, UK; Centre Georges Pompidou, Paris, France; Mori Art Museum, Tokyo, Japan; Moderna Museet, Stockholm, Sweden; Johannesburg Art Gallery, Johannesburg, South Africa

2004

A Grain of Dust, A Drop of Water, 5th Gwangju Biennale, Gwangju, South Korea
Intelligence Now! October Gallery, London, UK

2003

Africa Informs, October Gallery, London, UK
Biennale of Ceramics in Contemporary Art, Villa Groppallo, Vado Ligure, Italy
Transfer(t)s, Palais de Beaux Arts, Brussels, Belgium
Homage to Asele, National Museum Lagos, Lagos, Nigeria
Selected Works, Skoto Gallery, New York, USA

2002

The Independent, Liverpool Biennial of Contemporary Art, Liverpool, UK

2001 - 2002

The Happy Face of Globalization, 1st Albissola Ceramics Biennale, Albissola, Italy; Musée Ariana, Geneva, Switzerland

2001

El Tiempo de Africa, Centro Atlantico Arte Moderno, Las Palmas, Canary Islands; Consejería de Cultura de Comunidad, Madrid, Spain
Encounters with the Contemporary, National Museum of African Art, Smithsonian Institution, Washington, D.C., USA
Africas: The Artist and the City, Centre de Cultura Contemporània de Barcelona (CCCB), Barcelona, Spain
News from the Front, October Gallery, London, UK
Jazz and Visual Improvisations, Katonah Museum of Art, Katonah, New York, USA
Ebony Soliloquy: A Five Year Retrospective (1996-2001), Stella Jones Gallery, New Orleans, USA
Messagers de la Terre, Rur'Art– Espace d'Art Contemporain d'Lycée Agricole Xavier Bernard, Rouille, France

1999

New Colours From Old Worlds, October Gallery, London, UK
The Transvangarde, October Gallery, London, UK
Les Champs de la Sculpture, Champs Elysées, Paris, France
Contemporary Art from West Africa, October Gallery, London, UK

1998

7 Triennale der Kleineplastik, Stuttgart, Germany
9th Osaka Sculpture Triennale, Osaka, Japan
Riddle of the Spirits - Twelve African Artists, Skoto Gallery, New York, USA

1997

The Poetics of Line: Seven Artists of the Nsukka Group, National Museum of African Art, Smithsonian Institution, Washington D.C., USA
Free Form and Precision, Contemporary African Art Gallery, New York, USA

1996

Container '96: Art Across Oceans, Langelinie, Copenhagen, Denmark
Transvangarde, October Gallery, London, UK
Images of Africa, Torpedohallen, Copenhagen, Denmark
Africana, Sala 1, Rome, Italy
Transforms, October Gallery, London, UK
Group Exhibition, Avant-Garde Gallery, Kaduna, Nigeria
El Anatsui & Tesfaye Tessema, Contemporary African Gallery, New York, USA
El Anatsui & Sol Le Witt, Skoto Gallery, New York, USA

1995 - 1996

An Inside Story - African Art of our Time, Setagaya Art Museum, Tokyo; Tokushima Modern Art Museum, Tokushima; Himeji City Museum of Arts, Himeji; Koriyama City Museum of Art, Koriyama; Marugame Inokuma-Genichiro Museum of Contemporary Art (MIMOCA), Marugame; Museum of Fine Arts, Gifu, Japan

1995

AKA '95, Bona Gallery, Enugu; Didi Museum, Lagos, Nigeria
Contemporary African Art, World Intellectual Property Organisation Headquarters, Geneva, Switzerland
6th Osaka Sculpture Triennale, Osaka, Japan

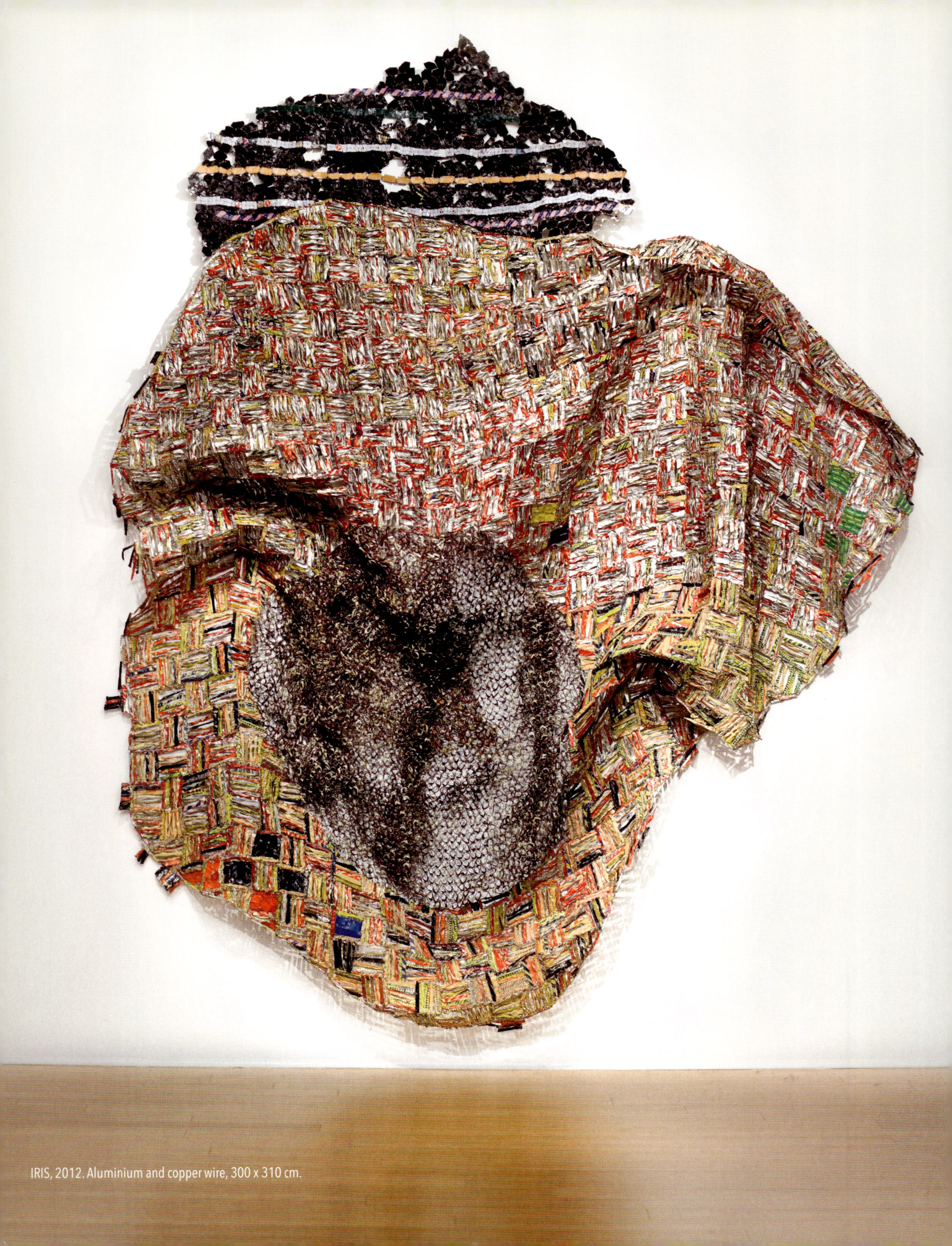

IRIS, 2012. Aluminium and copper wire, 300 x 310 cm.

1995

Seven Stories about Modern Art in Africa, Whitechapel Gallery, London, UK; Malmö Konsthall, Malmö, Sweden
Configura 2, Erfurt, Germany
The Right to Hope, Johannesburg Gallery, Johannesburg, South Africa; touring to Cairo; Amman; Gaza; Jerusalem; Tel Aviv
Africus, 1st Johannesburg Biennale, Johannesburg, South Africa
Uli Art– Master Works, Skoto Gallery, NY, USA

1994

Arte/ Sociedad/ Reflexion, 5th Havana Biennale, Havana, Cuba
AKA '94, Bona Gallery, Enugu; Didi Museum, Lagos, Nigeria

1993

New Currents '93 - Avant-Garde Nigerian Art, Didi Museum, Lagos, Nigeria
Six African Artists, October Gallery, London, UK
AKA '93, Bona Gallery, Enugu; Didi Museum, Lagos, Nigeria

1992

Arte Amazonas, Modern Art Museum, Rio de Janeiro, Brazil; traveled as: *Klima Global* to Staatliche Kunalle, Berlin; Ludwig Forum, Aachen, Germany
AKA '92, Bona Gallery, Enugu and Didi Museum, Lagos, Nigeria
Begegnung mit den Anderen, University of Kassel, Kassel, Germany

1991

El Desafi de Colonization, 4th Havana Biennale, Havana, Cuba
South of the World, Galleria d'Arte Contemporanea, Marsala, Italy
AKA '91, Bona Gallery, Enugu; Goethe-Institut, Lagos, Nigeria
Works by a Group of African Artists, The World Bank Art Society Gallery, World Bank Headquarters, Washington D.C., USA
The Sculptor's Guild of Nigeria Inaugural Exhibition, Murtala Mohammed Park, Enugu, Nigeria

1990

Five Contemporary African Artists, 44th Venice Biennale, Venice, Italy
The Calabash 1st Art Exhibition, The Calabash, Lagos, Nigeria
AKA '90, The Presicential Hotel, Enugu; Goethe-Insitut, Lagos, Nigeria
Achebe Celebration Exhibition, Continuing Education Centre, University of Nigeria, Nsukka, Nigeria
Contemporary African Artists: Changing Tradition, The Studio Museum in Harlem, New York; Afro-American Historical and Cultural Museum, Philadelphia; Chicago Public Library Cultural Centre, Chicago; Washington Project for the Arts, Washington D.C.; Museum of the National Center of African-American Artists, Boston, USA

1989

Zeitgenössische Nigerianische Kunst, Bonn, Bocholt and Mönchengladbach, Germany

1988

Walls and Gates - El Anatsui & Liz Willis, Avant-Garde Gallery, Kaduna, Nigeria
Thoughts and Processes - El Anatsui & Ndubisi Onah, The Italian Cultural Institute, Lagos, Nigeria
AKA '88, Nigerian Union of Journalists' Press Centre, Enugu; Contemporary Art Gallery, Institute of African Studies, Nsukka; National Gallery of Crafts and Design, Lagos, Nigeria

1987

AKA '87, The Presidential Hotel, Enugu; National Gallery of Crafts and Design, Lagos, Nigeria
Original Prints from the 3rd Nsukka Workshop, University of Nigeria, Nsukka and Goethe-Institut, Lagos, Nigeria

1986

AKA '86 - Inaugural Exhibition of the AKA Circle of Artists, the French Centre, Enugu and Goethe-Institut, Lagos, Nigeria
Nigerian-German Prints, University of Nigeria, Nsukka; Franco-German Auditorium, Lagos, Nigeria

1983

Four Contemporary African Artists, Mintec Gallery, Port Harcourt, Nigeria

1982

Okike 10th Anniversary Exhibition, University of Nigeria, Nsukka, Nigeria

1981

Drawing on the World, Billingham Art Gallery, Billingham; Middlesborough Art Gallery, Middlesborough and the House of Commons Gallery, London, UK

1979

Christian Arts in Nigeria, Holy Trinity Cathedral Hall, Onitsha, Nigeria
The Nsukka School, Art Gallery of the Rivers State Council for Arts and Culture, Port Harcourt, Nigeria

1975

Fabric Wall Hangings, Burnt Wooden Wall Plaques, The Institute of African Studies, University of Nigeria, Nsukka, Nigeria

1974

Tekarts Expo 5, National Arts Centre, Accra; Specialist Training College, Winneba, Ghana

1969 - 1970

Ghana National Collection, National Arts Centre, Accra, Ghana; National Museum of African Art, Smithsonian Institution, Washington, D.C., USA

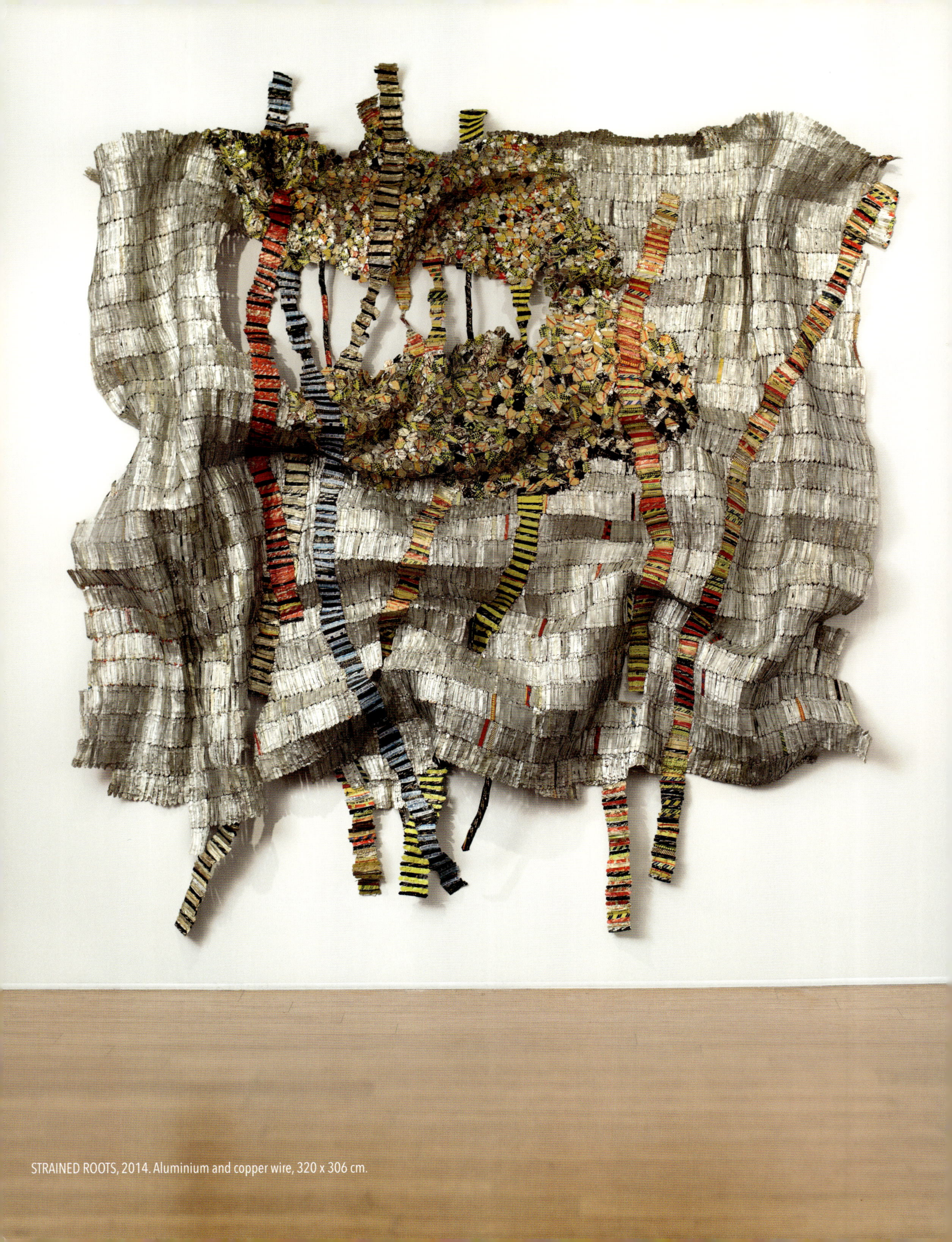

STRAINED ROOTS, 2014. Aluminium and copper wire, 320 x 306 cm.

Public Collections

African Studies Gallery, University of Nigeria, Nsukka, Nigeria
Akron Art Museum, Akron, Ohio, USA
Asele Institute, Nimo, Nigeria
Bill and Melinda Gates Foundation, Seattle, Washington, USA
The Blanton Museum, University of Texas, Austin, Texas, USA
The British Museum, London, UK
The Brooklyn Museum, Brooklyn, New York, USA
The Carnegie Endowment for International Peace, Washington D.C., USA
Centre Georges Pomipdou, Paris, France
Clarks International Art Collection, Somerset, UK
ConocoPhillips, Houston, Texas, USA
De Young Museum, San Francisco, USA
Denver Art Museum, Colorado, USA
Diamond Bank of Nigeria, Victoria Island, Lagos, Nigeria
Eden Project, Cornwall, UK
Embassy of Ghana, Copenhagen, Denmark
Fowler Museum, University of California, Los Angeles, USA
French Cultural Centre, Lagos, Nigeria
Guggenheim Abu Dhabi, Abu Dhabi, UAE
The Hammermill Collection, Hellebaek, Helsingør, Denmark
Hood Museum of Art, Hanover, New Hampshire, USA
Indianapolis Museum of Art, Indianapolis, Indiana, USA
International Peoples' College, Helsingør, Denmark
Iwalewa-Haus, University of Bayreuth, Bayreuth, Germany
Jordan National Gallery of Arts, Amman, Jordan
Los Angeles County Museum of Art, California, USA
Missoni, Milan, Italy
The Metropolitan Museum of Art, New York, NY, USA
Musée Ariana, Geneva, Switzerland
Museum of Art, University of Iowa, Iowa City, Iowa, USA
Museum Kunstpalast, Düsseldorf, Germany
National Museum of African Art, Smithsonian Institution, Washington D.C., USA
The Museum of Modern Art, New York, USA
The National Gallery of Art, Lagos, Nigeria
The Nelson-Atkins Museum, Kansas City, Missouri, USA
The Newark Museum, New Jersey, USA
Novartis Campus, Basel, Switzerland
North Carolina Museum of Art, Raleigh, North Carolina, USA
Osaka Foundation of Culture, Osaka, Japan
Princeton University Art Museum, Princeton NJ, USA
Royal Ontario Museum, Toronto, Canada
Rubell Family Collection, Miami, FL, USA
Saint Louis Art Museum, St. Louis, MO, USA
Samuel P. Harn Museum of Art, Gainesville, Florida, USA
Setagaya Art Museum, Tokyo, Japan
Tate Modern, London, UK
UNAIDS, Geneva, Switzerland
The World Bank Art Collection, Washington D.C., USA
21st Century Museum of Contemporary Art, Kanagawa, Japan

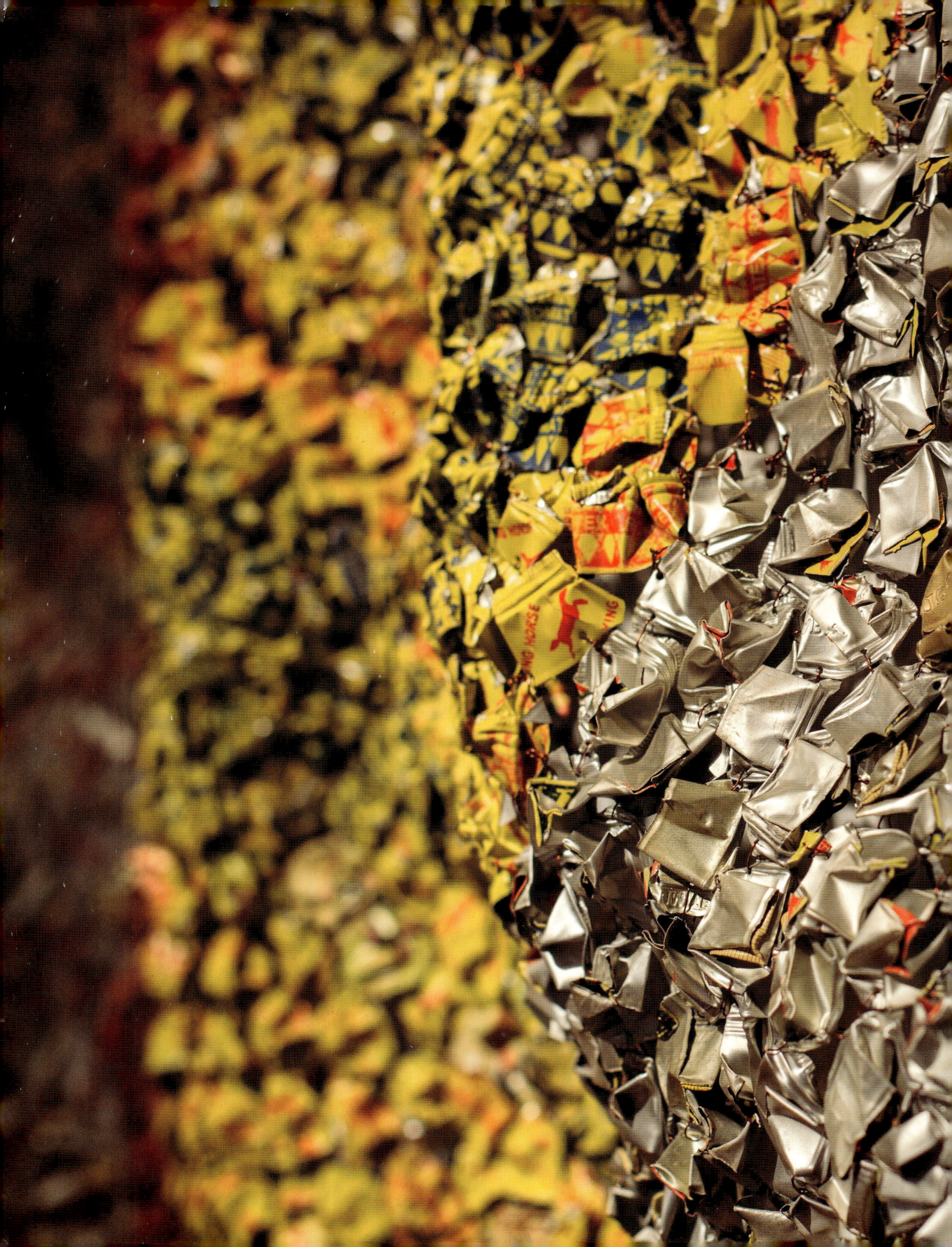